THE
BENEFITS
OF AN
ENEMY

FRANK SANTORA

D1468836

Frank Santora Ministries
600 Danbury Road
New Milford, CT 06776
www.franksantora.cc

ISBN: 9781982960247
Printed in the United States of America
©2018 by Frank Santora
All Rights Reserved.

INTRODUCTION

Fight the good fight of faith, lay hold on eternal life, to which you were also called and have confessed the good confession in the presence of many witnesses.
1 Timothy 6:12

Whether you know it or not, whether you like it or not, and whether you are ready or not...the truth is, you and I are in a real fight against a spiritual enemy. That enemy, the devil, has rallied demonic forces and has engineered oppressive situations against you to kill you, steal everything precious to you, and destroy your destiny in Christ.

In the kingdom of God, there is no such thing as passivity; everyone is a warrior and has received a call to duty. Our warfare is not only for self-defense, but to ensure that we become what God has destined for us because many people may ultimately be touched by our lives.

In the Kingdom of God, there is no such thing as a conscientious objector! You can't sit back on your 'blessed assurance' and take the fatalistic attitude that whatever will be will be and expect to live the abundant life Jesus promises to give us in John 10:10. If you do, the devil will kick the snot out of you. The truth is, you must fight in order to win your battles; and if you do fight, you can be certain that you will win them.

No matter how long you have been in Christ, you will face battles in this life. It doesn't matter whether your battle is a person, a situation, a hang up or a bad habit; they are the work of the enemy. In order to overcome and walk in victory, you must pick up your sword and fight.

The enemy is real, and the battles are relentless. Don't be discouraged because there are also very real benefits to having an enemy. In fact, to become everything you are meant to be in Christ, it is absolutely necessary to have an enemy.

Now, that may seem a bit counter-intuitive, or perhaps it messes with your theology some. When most of us think of enemies, we don't want them! Our view of an enemy is someone or something that causes grief, heartache, pain, turmoil or stress to enter our lives.

Moreover, don't most of us try to avoid having enemies, to turn the other cheek and make peace?

After all the scripture does tell us things like:

> You have heard that it was said, "You shall love your neighbor and hate your enemy." But I say to you, love your enemies, bless those who curse you, do good to those who hate you, and pray for those who spitefully use you and persecute you, that you may be sons of your Father in heaven;...
> Matthew 5:43-45a

The Apostle Paul also instructed us in this way in the Book of Romans:

> If it is possible, as far as it depends on you, live at peace with everyone.

But for true spiritual maturity to occur, for you to grow more like Christ and progress from glory to glory in order to become everything God wants you to be, you need an enemy! Too few of us realize that the struggle against our adversity is something that works God's best in us.

In fact, our enemies are just as essential as our friends. When we have enemies, it means we are in the game!

I. Your Ticket to Being Blessed

In Matthew Chapter 5, Jesus gives the greatest sermon ever preached, the

Sermon on the Mount. In it, He describes the famous "beatitudes" or the circumstances under which you and I can find the greatest blessing in life.

Beginning in verse 10, He says:

Blessed are those who are persecuted because of righteousness, for theirs is the kingdom of heaven. Blessed are you when people insult you, persecute you and falsely say all kinds of evil against you because of me. Rejoice and be glad, because great is your reward in heaven, for in the same way they persecuted the prophets who were before you.
Matthew 5:10-11 NIV

Blessed are those, (that is, "empowered") are those to prosper in every area of life!

Doesn't it seem the scripture is saying that in order for you and I to be blessed (empowered), we must be persecuted, insulted, falsely accused and be spoken evil of? And the only way that can happen is if we have an enemy coming against us in some way. In Matthew 5:44, Jesus says to "Love your enemies, bless those who curse you, do good to those who hate you..." Why should we love our enemies and do good to our enemies? Because they are our ticket to the blessed life!

A Conversation with Peter

It's interesting how Jesus viewed his friends and his enemies.

In Matthew 16, Jesus had a conversation with his disciple and friend, Peter, that begins amazingly well. In this conversation, Jesus calls him blessed, changed his name and declared, "You are a rock and I will use you to build my church".

But when Jesus tells the disciples that He must go to Jerusalem, suffer many things at the hands of the chief priests, be killed and be resurrected, Pete jumps to his feet with bravado and says, "Never Lord, this won't happen to you!"

And then is gets really interesting. Turning to this same disciple that He declared would build His church, Jesus shuts him down and says,

"Get behind me, Satan! You are a stumbling block to me; you do not have in mind the concerns of God, but merely human concerns."
Matthew 16:23 NIV

Jesus tells his friend, Peter, that at that moment, he was His enemy, because Peter was attempting to steer Jesus away from His mission and His destiny.

A Conversation with Judas

Now, compare this conversation between Peter and Jesus, with the infamous conversation Jesus had with Judas Iscariot a little later.

Judas, also a disciple of Jesus, made a decision to betray Jesus for thirty pieces of silver. He led the chief priests and Temple Guard to arrest Jesus in the middle of the night. As the authorities approached the camp, Judas walks up to Jesus to identify Him, and gives Jesus a big, phony, hypocritical, backstabbing kiss on the cheek.

To which Jesus responds:

"Do what you came for, friend."
Matthew 26:50 NIV

Whaz up, Jesus?

He calls His friend, His enemy, and His enemy, His friend!

Jesus knew the truth of the matter. To fulfill His destiny, to pay the price of sin and bring sons and daughters into the Kingdom of God, Jesus *needed* Judas to betray Him. He needed that enemy to set in motion the circumstances that would cause Him to defeat death, hell and the grave. He needed the enemy, the persecution and the suffering, in order to be able to a Redeemed Church into heaven for eternity! And in that moment, the enemy Judas caused all this blessing to come to Jesus.

In the very same way, we need an enemy to be everything that He has designed us to be in order to fulfill every work He has set before us. Clearly, Jesus knew that our enemies were our tickets to the blessed life.

A Case Study: Nehemiah

The book of Nehemiah gives us a great example of this principle put into action. Nehemiah was the cupbearer of King Artaxerxes of Persia. It was his job to "taste test" any drink set before the King. If it was poisoned, Nehemiah would drink it first and die, protecting the king's life. In short, Nehemiah's life was considered to be disposable.

While serving King Artaxerxes in that position, Nehemiah received word that the walls of his hometown city, Jerusalem, were in ruin and the gates had been burned to the ground. The citizens of Jerusalem, his family and friends, were unprotected from their many enemies. When Nehemiah heard this, he began to weep for his people and God instructed him to go on a divine assignment, to rally the people to rebuild the walls of the city.

Through a series of divinely orchestrated events, Nehemiah received permission from King Artaxerxes to leave Persia and go fulfill his divine assignment.

II. Your Enemy Is Your Evidence

When you encounter an enemy in your life, you suddenly have verifiable evidence that you are on the right track and that you matter more than you think! It's inevitable that as you begin to walk in the will of God and to move toward your destiny in Christ, enemies in the form of people, negative circumstances and unexpected events, are sent to hinder you and discourage you into giving up.

Nehemiah was in the will of God, and he experienced a miracle getting permission to leave Persia. But as is always the case whenever you are on assignment from God, enemies appeared to oppose Nehemiah in Jerusalem. Sanballat, the governor of Samaria, Tobiah, an Ammonite, and a motley crew of others arose to oppose and stop Nehemiah.

When Sanballat heard that we were rebuilding the wall, he became angry and was greatly incensed. He

ridiculed the Jews, and in the presence of his associates and the army of Samaria, he said, "What are those feeble Jews doing? Will they restore their wall? Will they offer sacrifices? Will they finish in a day? Can they bring the stones back to life from those heaps of rubble—burned as they are?" Tobiah the Ammonite, who was at his side, said, "What they are building—even a fox climbing up on it would break down their wall of stones!"
Nehemiah 4:1-3 NIV

The devil sent Sanballat to hinder and discourage Nehemiah, but in truth, Sanballat was a sign that Nehemiah was right smack in the middle of God's will. There's no getting around it: anytime we are doing what God wants us to, there will be opposition!

So be encouraged, opposition is not a sign that something's wrong with you, it's a sign that something is right with you! It's a sign that you matter to God, that God trusts you and has enlisted you to carry out a part of His divine plan.

Make this a victory in your mindset today: when an enemy arises in your life, begin to give God glory for that sign of significance! Instead of complaining to family and friends about the person or situation, say "Thank you, Lord, for confirming to me that I'm on the right track!"

For example, wouldn't it be amazing if, when the enemy of sickness shows up, instead Googling our symptoms in a panic, we would simply declare, "Thank you,

Lord! I can see that I matter so much, the devil is trying to take me out!"

Or when the enemy of depression shows up...instead of crying ourselves to sleep at night, we would say, "Thank you, Lord! I can tell that I matter so much, the devil is trying to keep me down!"

And when the enemy of adverse circumstances shows up and we want to call the lawyer...instead, we would say, "Thank you, Lord! I now know for sure that I matter so much, the devil is trying to keep me bound, box me in, shut me down and knock me out!"

Just imagine how we, the children of God, would freak out the devil if, anytime an enemy showed up, we simply said,

"Hello, friend! It's good to see you, 'cause I needed some confirmation that I was still on the right track!"

III. The Benefits of an Enemy

Sanballat was the Governor of Samaria, a neighboring nation that hated the Jews. Sanballat wanted to keep the Jews exposed by broken city walls and bound by fear. He knew that if the walls surrounding Jerusalem were rebuilt, God's people would rise up again and the city would become a bustling, economic hub for the region... and it would eventually hurt Samaria's bottom line.

In the same way, your spiritual enemy, the devil, is afraid of your success and will try to stop you. But be of good cheer, because like Nehemiah and Sanballat, God will use your enemy to be part of your success!

Notice how the enemy attacked Nehemiah with ridicule and criticism.

- *What are these feeble Jews doing? (meaning... you're not good enough!)*
- *If a fox jumps on the wall they are rebuilding, it will fall! (meaning... what you're doing isn't good enough!)*

Isn't that just like the enemy to harass you, ridicule you and criticize you?

- You can't...
- You're not able...

- You're stupid...
- You're a poor excuse for a parent...
- You're a disgrace for a husband...
- You're too fat...
- You're too skinny...
- You're too U.G.L.Y...
  You ain't got no alibi... You're ugly...
  hey hey,
  You're ugly!

Child of God, when the enemy ridicules you and criticizes you, just say, "Thank you, friend! You're my ticket to the blessed life because Jesus said, 'Blessed are you when people insult you, persecute you, and falsely say all kinds of evil against you because of me.'"

How does God work that transformation in us, to turn all these negative situations in our lives around for our good?

A. Enemies Push Us to Pray

Listen to the cry of Nehemiah's heart...

> *Hear us, our God, for we are despised.*
> *Nehemiah 4:4 NIV*

Notice that Nehemiah's response to the appearance of these enemies was to reach out to God in prayer.

In the same way, have you ever noticed how much more you pray when an enemy shows up to oppose you in your life, and how little you pray (by comparison, that is) when everything is going along okay?

It seems our relationship with God and devotional time increases, or even gets back on track, when an enemy shows up. And we sometimes go through spiritual seasons nearly void of intimate prayer... only to have that precious communion with God restored because an enemy showed up.

And if we believe in what prayer is and what prayer does...

- that prayer works
- that prayer saves
- that prayer empowers
- that prayer fills us with Godly wisdom which we would otherwise not know
- that prayer changes things
- that prayer impregnates us with God's strength

- that prayer lifts the burden off us and places it on God
- that prayer fills us with joy and changes our countenance
- that prayer lifts us from the doldrums of depression and worry
- that prayer prepares the way for our success
- that prayer puts up a hedge of protection around us
- that prayer frustrates the plans of the enemy
- and that prayer allows God to interfere in our affairs

If we believe in what prayer is and what prayer does, then isn't the appearance of an enemy in our lives a good thing... because it's that enemy that often pushes us to prayer!

Now look at verse 9. It says,

But we prayed to our God, and because of them we set up a guard against them day and night.
Nehemiah 4:9

We prayed because of them.

We prayed... because of them.

We are blessed when we pray, and we prayed *because of* our enemies!

B. Enemies Push Us to Rely on God

We know from John 10:10, that the devil's objective against us is to kill, steal and destroy. To do that, he will send people and situations our way that cause us to experience pain. But pain is a change agent that deepens our dependence on God. When we hurt, we run to God because we want to stop hurting.

When we go to God because of the pain, we go with a heart more willing to do whatever He asks of us, because we want the pain to go away. And so the pain, caused by the enemy, winds up being an instrument that breaks our independent spirits and causes us to rely on God as we should.

In the remote, mountainous regions of Kazakhstan and Kyrgyzstan, live men who train eagles for hunting, a centuries-old practice. The method for training these majestic birds, however cruel it may seem, is so ancient it has become ritual, a tradition passed from father to son. Captured when newly hatched or barely out of the nest, a young bird is immediately blinded with a hood. Unable to see, it's kept in a cage designed to rock without ceasing. Disoriented and constantly having to maintain its balance, the young bird is unable to sleep. The hunter does not feed the bird for up to three days, only chanting and singing to it endlessly, so that the bird tunes its hearing to the master's voice. After three days, the hunter strokes the bird, feeding it by hand, continuing to talk to it. Soon the relationship between eagle and hunter becomes unbreakable, the bird relying solely on its new master for everything. The bird's loyalty is fierce and lifelong—the hunter doesn't even need a leash or hood. The eagle will always return to its master.[1]

It's interesting that the Bible compares the people of God to eagles. Pain is part of the process that helps us become as eagles, flying higher in life. And it requires our complete reliance and dependence upon God.

Jabez, Too

You might recall the story of Jabez in 1 Chronicles and the now-famous prayer he prayed which changed his life.

> And Jabez called on the God of Israel saying, "Oh, that You would bless me indeed, and enlarge my territory, that Your hand would be with me, and that You would keep me from evil, that I may not cause pain!" So God granted him what he requested.
> 1 Chronicles 4:10

Jabez means "pain" That's what his mother named him! Surely he took quite a lot of ribbing throughout his life, for having that name.

So what caused him to pray this kind of prayer of dependence and reliance on

God? Pain! And what is the primary cause of pain in our lives – our enemies.

When an enemy causes pain in your life, look that enemy in the eye and say, just like Jesus, "Do what you came for, friend. Your pain is my push from self-reliance to God-dependence, and it just might push me to pray a transformational prayer in which God will grant me what I request...and my life will change!"

C. Enemies Push Us to Become Our Best

Haven't we all benefited in life by focusing and setting our mind to really do something. We know the difference that makes. Setting our mind to do something causes us to train harder, work longer, refuse to take 'no' for an answer, be persistent, and keep on going.

Under Nehemiah's leadership, in the face of enemy opposition the people of Jerusalem joined together and set their minds on accomplishing the job of rebuilding the city walls.

So we built the wall, and the entire wall was joined together up to half its height, for the people had a mind to work.
Nehemiah 4:6

When we decide to do it and then put our mind to doing it, we become an unstoppable force; setting our mind to do something brings out the best in us!

In fact, the word "repent" in the Bible literally means to have a change of mind. Contrary to popular belief repentance is much more than turning from sin, it's changing your mind about sin. And when you change your mind about something the rest of you follows.

Setting My Mind to Lose Weight

I remember years ago I decided to set my mind to lose weight. I was 262 lbs, depressed, lethargic and uninspired.

One morning in prayer God spoke to me about my assignment over the next ten years and how taxing it was going to be on my body. Immediately the Holy Spirit said to me, ...

if you are going to fulfill what the Father just spoke to you – you are going to have to get in shape!

With that word, I set my mind to lose weight. No longer was losing weight a "vanity" issue for me...it was now a "destiny" issue for me. It was about being ready and equipped to do God's work.

That revelation caused me to set my mind to getting in shape. Over the next three months, I lost 70 lbs! The difficulty of my journey became the "enemy" that changed my mindset, and that mindset brought out the best in me physically.

Now, have you ever noticed how an enemy can push you to "set your face like flint" to do something and refuse to turn back?

For example, remember the movie "Rocky IV." What caused Rocky to go to Russia and train like he did to defeat Ivan Drago? What caused him to sacrifice time away from his family? What caused him to put his body through that kind of pre-fight training? What was it that brought out the best in Rocky?

Drago became his enemy because he had killed Rocky's friend, Apollo; and it caused Rocky to set his mind to defeat Drago.

Have you ever noticed how, as soon as someone gets divorced they start looking good? They start wearing nice clothes and cleaning up and fixing their hair and losing weight? Why? Their ex-spouse becomes their enemy and they set their mind to make them realize what they've lost!

In the same way, an enemy can cause us to stay spiritually fit, to stay on our game. It brings out winning attributes like creativity, resilience, persistence and perseverance. And it also causes us to shore up any weaknesses or infirmities and close any gaps in our lives.

Image Is Everything

But most importantly, having an enemy causes us to become our best, because adversity makes us glorious!

> For our light affliction, which is but for a moment, is working for us a far more exceeding and eternal weight of glory.
> 2 Corinthians 4:17

The word "glory" literally means "to reflect or to look like". A better way of saying it would be to have an image change.

When Hollywood executives want to turn someone into a movie star or a celebrity, they focus on giving that person an image change. Then they make sure that image is played out to the max.

In much the same way, that's what God does for us when He makes us into a star in His kingdom; He gives us an image change and then focuses on making that image brighter and brighter

What is that image that God transforms us into? It is the image of His Son, Jesus Christ!

And how does that image get stronger and stronger? God uses the affliction that the enemy throws our way to grow our glory.

Till They See the Reflection

It takes time, patience, and an extremely hot fire to refine silver and gold. The impurities are painstakingly removed by repeating the refining process, each time making the metal more and more pure. Ultimately, the way that a silversmith or goldsmith knows it's time to take the precious metal out of the fires of purification is when they can see their image reflected in the surface of the liquefied metal.

The enemy may mean for his affliction to take you out, but God will use that affliction to transform you, just like the silversmith transforms silver and the goldsmith refines gold.

Shadrach, Meshach, and Abednego

Remember the story of the Hebrew boys who refused to bow to the egomaniac King of Babylon, who thought himself to be a god to be worshipped? This king became so enraged, he ordered the boys to be burned alive in the hottest furnace he could muster. But what did the king see after he threw Shadrach, Meshach and Abednego into the fire?

He asked his servants, "Didn't we only throw three men into the furnace?"

They said, "Yes."

"Look!" he answered, *"I see four men loose, walking in the midst of the fire; and they are not hurt, and the form of the fourth is like the Son of God."*
Daniel 3:25

The fire of affliction caused the image of Christ to come shining forth from them!

The next time your spiritual enemy sends affliction, tell him, "Do what you came to do, because it will only bring out the best in me!"

The Rest of the Nehemiah's Story:
Cliff Notes Version

- Nehemiah continues to rebuild the wall and Sanballat continues to try to stop his progress

- Sanballat threatens Nehemiah and the people, threatening to sneak up on them while they are working and kill them
- Since Nehemiah was given permission by the King of Persia to rebuild the walls, Sanballat had no real authority to kill Nehemiah or the people working with him

Lesson: The devil may try to rock your world and threaten you... but he has no real authority over you because you are a King's kid!

- The people get discouraged when they hit the half way point; the work is hard and they think Sanballat is going to attack

- They are working with a sword in one hand and a trowel in the other
- They aren't getting any sleep: they are laborers by day and guards by night
- Nehemiah encourages them and rallies them to keep on going

Lesson: Work hard, but always have the Sword of the Spirit (which is the Word of God) ready to defeat any onslaught of the enemy.

The people of Jerusalem got tired, discouraged and wanted to stop half-way through the job. But Nehemiah rallied them to keep going, saying:

- Don't stop half way there
- Don't stop when you've come so far

- You are closer to your breakthrough than you think
- You have crossed the midway point; it will take you more energy to go back than to keep fighting
- Fight to the end, the reward is worth it!

Lesson: *The enemy knows the only way he can win is if he gets you to quit!*

- The people start fighting over the financial burdens they are carrying from the taxes
- Nehemiah goes to the authorities on behalf of the people and gets them to release the people of their financial burdens
- Finally, the wall is rebuilt, Jerusalem is safe, and the people rejoice and throw a party!

Promotion Happens

But then something happens that changes everything for Nehemiah.

> *Moreover, from the time that I was appointed to be their governor in the land of Judah, from the twentieth year until the thirty-second year of King Artaxerxes...*
> Nehemiah 5:14

Because Nehemiah answered the call of God and committed to fulfill his assignment, an enemy showed up which pushed Nehemiah to pray and rely on God and brought out the best in him... Nehemiah was now ready to become governor of the land of Judah!

From disposable cup bearer to indispensible governor of the tribe from which Jesus would come!

D. Enemies Push Us Toward the Next Promotion

We must realize that the arrival of an enemy signals that a change is coming. The current season is coming to an end, and a new season of greater things is dawning. An enemy is a sign of exit from one level and the entrance into another level. Your friends can encourage you, and your family can stand by you, but only your enemy can promote you!

The Bible is full of examples:

- Goliath pushed David into position for the throne of Israel
- Pharaoh pushed Moses out of hiding to become Israel's Deliverer
- Haman pushed Esther to go before the king to rescue her people from destruction
- Potiphar's wife pushed Joseph into prison, where he had a divine appointment to become Prime Minister over Egypt
- And Judas pushed Jesus to the cross, giving Him a Name that is above every name!

You may see your enemy as a stopping point, but God sees your enemy as a stepping stool! Anytime someone's influence pushes you into promotion, their presence is necessary in your life. And now you know why it says in Romans,

> And we know that all things work together for good to those who love God, to those who are the called according to His purpose.
> Romans 8:28

Now you know why the Apostle Paul said in Philippians,

> ...being confident of this very thing, that He who has begun a good work in you will complete it until the day of Jesus Christ;...
> Philippians 1:6

Now you know why the Prophet Isaiah said,

No weapon formed against you shall prosper, and every tongue which rises against you in judgment you shall condemn. This is the heritage of the servants of the LORD,...
Isaiah 54:17

And now you know why Jesus looked at Judas and said, "Do what you've come to do, friend!"

Child of God, your enemy may intend to work against you but the God of the Universe will use him to work for you!

Final Thoughts: *The enemy does leave, doesn't he?*

Now you would think the enemy would go away; after all, Nehemiah won!

- Nehemiah was promoted to governor
- Nehemiah reached the pinnacle of his career
- He experienced the promised blessing
- His assignment from God was complete
- The walls of Jerusalem were securely rebuilt
- The nation of Israel turned back to God

But Nehemiah 6:1-2 says:

Now it happened when Sanballat, Tobiah, Geshem the Arab, and the rest of our enemies heard that I had rebuilt the wall, and that there were no breaks left in it (though at that time I had not hung the doors in the gates), that Sanballat and Geshem

sent to me, saying, "Come, let us
meet together among the villages in
the plain of Ono." But they thought
to do me harm.
Nehemiah 6:1-2

After all that and the hard won victory of Nehemiah, why didn't the enemy go away? Because even after the walls were rebuilt, God wasn't done with Nehemiah yet; He had another level of glory for Nehemiah to experience!

Why doesn't the enemy go away after you fought the good fight of faith and received your healing?

Why doesn't the enemy go away after you fought, prayed, and got financial breakthrough?

Why doesn't the enemy go away after you invested time and attention, and saw your marriage saved?

Why doesn't the enemy go away after you suffered and struggled and beat the addiction?

Just like Nehemiah, God is not done with you either; He has another level of blessedness and influence for you to experience, and if that's going to happen, you too will need an enemy!

1 Stephen Kinzer, "Bokonbayeva Journal; God of Birds, but Scourge of Foxes and Badgers," *New York Times*, November 4, 1999.

Made in the USA
Middletown, DE
16 May 2021